THE OMEGA FILES

SHORT STORIES

Some strange things happen in this world. You hear all kinds of frightening stories. But are they true? Who do you believe? Some stories never get into the newspapers, because governments want to keep them secret. And these are the stories in the Omega Files.

How many people know about the Omega Files? Not many – perhaps no more than thirty people in Brussels. Hawker and Jude know about them, because they bring back a lot of the stories that go into the Files. They have interesting lives. One day they're in London, talking to a young man. He has a strange story to tell them, about a drug company, but is it true? Another day they go to Scotland, to look for a monster in Loch Ness, but of course, there *are* no monsters – are there? Another time they're on an island in the Pacific Ocean, where everybody is talking about a spaceship. But where is this spaceship? And who has actually seen it?

It's all there, in the Omega Files.

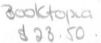

OXFORD BOOKWORMS LIBRARY
Fantasy & Horror

The Omega Files

SHORT STORIES

Stage 1 (400 headwords)

Series Editor: Jennifer Bassett
Founder Editor: Tricia Hedge
Activities Editors: Jennifer Bassett and Christine Lindop

JENNIFER BASSETT

The Omega Files

SHORT STORIES

Illustrated by
Paul Dickinson

OXFORD UNIVERSITY PRESS

OXFORD

UNIVERSITY PRESS

Great Clarendon Street, Oxford OX2 6DP

Oxford University Press is a department of the University of Oxford.
It furthers the University's objective of excellence in research, scholarship,
and education by publishing worldwide in

Oxford New York

Auckland Cape Town Dar es Salaam Hong Kong Karachi
Kuala Lumpur Madrid Melbourne Mexico City Nairobi
New Delhi Shanghai Taipei Toronto

With offices in

Argentina Austria Brazil Chile Czech Republic France Greece
Guatemala Hungary Italy Japan Poland Portugal Singapore
South Korea Switzerland Thailand Turkey Ukraine Vietnam

OXFORD and OXFORD ENGLISH are registered trade marks of
Oxford University Press in the UK and in certain other countries

ISBN 978 0 19 478913 4

A complete recording of this Bookworms edition of
The Omega Files is available on audio CD ISBN 978 0 19 478848 9

Printed in China

Word count (main text): 5830 words

For more information on the Oxford Bookworms Library,
visit www.oup.com/bookworms

In the early years Hawker and Jude travelled a lot. Brussels, Strasbourg, Rome, Delhi, Washington . . . North Africa, South America, Australia . . . No home, no family, just work. They worked for the top man in the Brussels office of EDI, and only for him. He was called Arla. Nobody knew his real name, or much about him. Some said he was Latvian; others said he was from another planet. He always gave the hard jobs to Hawker and Jude. The jobs with questions, but not many answers. The Omega Files.

When I met them, many years later, Hawker and Jude were about seventy years old. They lived very quietly, in a little white house on a Greek island. They went walking, swimming, fishing; they sat in the sun, and slept a lot.

At first, they didn't want to talk about their work.

'We can't,' said Jude. 'Our work was secret. It's all in the government files, and nobody can read them.'

'After thirty years,' I said, 'people can read all secret government files.'

'Not these files,' Hawker said. 'It's a hundred years before people can read the EDI files.'

I looked at them. 'But I don't need to read the files,' I said. 'I can get the stories from you.'

❑ ❑ ❑

And I did. Here are some of them . . .

CONTENTS

EDI
European Department of Intelligence

There were two of them. Hawker and Jude. They had no other names. Just Hawker and Jude. They were young, fast, and clever. They worked for EDI, in the European Government.

You know about the Americans' CIA and the Russians' KGB? Well, this was EDI – the European Department of Intelligence. Big secrets. Very strange secrets. The secrets of the Omega Files. They don't get into the newspapers, and most people never hear about them. Most people don't know anything about EDI.

1

CONTENTS

'There's a young man in London called Johnny Cook,' Arla said. 'He's about eighteen. He doesn't have a home, but he goes clubbing nearly every night. Those all-night dance clubs for young people. Here's a photograph of him.'

He put the photograph on the table, and Jude and Hawker looked at it.

'And?' Hawker said.

'He wants to sell a story to a newspaper,' Arla said. 'Some story about a drug company. Find him. Talk to him. What's his story? I want to know.'

Jude and Hawker took an afternoon plane from Brussels to London, and then went to a hotel.

'What are you going to wear tonight?' said Jude. 'Not those old jeans, please!'

'What's wrong with them?' Hawker said. 'We're going clubbing, not out to dinner at the Ritz Hotel.'

'Well, wear a different shirt, then. That one's dirty.'

'You can wash it for me,' Hawker said.

'Get lost!' said Jude.

They had dinner, watched television for an hour or

3

two, and then went out. It was a warm night, with a little rain now and then.

'London weather,' said Hawker.

They found a taxi with a young driver, and got in.

'Where to?' said the driver.

They found a taxi with a young driver, and got in.

'We want to go clubbing,' Jude said. 'Where's the best place this week? Do you know?'

'Bruno's,' the driver said. 'Or Garcia's, down by the river. Everybody's going there this week.'

'OK, let's go!' said Hawker.

They went to Garcia's first, then moved on to Bruno's. They found Johnny Cook in a third club, called Monty's. It was two o'clock in the morning.

'That's him, all right,' Hawker said. 'Look at his ear.'

Johnny Cook was tall and thin, with long yellow hair and two black earrings in his left ear.

'Johnny! Johnny Cook!' shouted Jude suddenly. She ran and put her arms round Johnny Cook's neck. 'Hi, Johnny! You remember me – Jude. We met last week, at Garcia's. You remember? Oh, this is my friend Hawker.'

'Hi, Johnny. Good to meet you,' said Hawker.

'Hi,' said Johnny Cook. He looked at Jude. 'Did we meet at Garcia's?'

'Of course we did,' laughed Jude. 'I was with Sara and Patti and the others, remember?'

'Oh. Yeah,' said Johnny. 'I remember.' He looked around. 'Are they here tonight?'

'No, it's just me and Hawker tonight,' said Jude. 'Come on, let's dance.'

They danced for two hours. Then they left with about ten other people, and went across the river to a new club.

'Don't these people ever go to bed?' said Hawker.

The music there was louder and the dancing was very
fast. After two more hours of dancing, Hawker was hot,
tired, and thirsty.

'I'm getting old,' he said to Jude. 'Don't these people
ever go to bed?'

'You're only twenty-five!' said Jude. 'That's not old.

And you can't stop yet. He's getting very friendly now, and we can take him to breakfast soon.'

At seven o'clock the club closed, and Jude and Hawker took Johnny back to their hotel. Jude picked up the phone and asked for three big breakfasts in the room.

Hawker took his shoes off. 'Ah, that's better,' he said. He looked at Johnny. 'How often do you go clubbing, Johnny? And what do you do in the daytime?'

'Not a lot. Sleep, usually. I go clubbing most nights.'

'Where do you live?' Hawker asked.

'On the streets,' said Johnny. 'When I'm rich, I'm going to get a boat and live on that.'

'Rich?' Jude said. 'Oh yes, we all want to be rich!'

'But I *am* going to be rich,' Johnny said. 'I've got a good story, see?' He laughed. 'I'm going to sell it. A newspaper wants to give me 100,000 Euros for it. They gave me 1,000 last month, and I'm going to get the other 99,000 very soon.'

'Great!' said Jude. 'So what's the story then, Johnny? Have some more coffee, and tell us all about it.'

'Well, you know the Tyler Drug Company?' Johnny began. 'They make drugs and medicines.'

'Yes,' Hawker said. 'It's a very big European company. They've got offices in all the big cities.'

'Yeah, that's right,' Johnny said. 'Well, they're taking young people off the streets, and using them for tests.'

Jude laughed. 'Nobody's going to believe that!' she said. 'Drug companies use animals, not people, for their tests. Some new drugs can be very dangerous at first. Nobody wants people to die from a new medicine!'

'It's true!' Johnny said angrily. 'Think about it. All those young homeless people in London. They sleep every night along the Strand, and other streets. Nobody wants to know them, nobody asks questions about them. They've got no home, no family, nothing.'

'But they've got legs,' Hawker said. 'They can run away.'

'You don't understand,' said Johnny. 'Listen. I *know*, because I was there! I live on the streets, right? And late one night, along the Strand, they came and took me and some other people – a boy and two girls. They wanted to help us, they said. Hot food, nice beds, new clothes – everything! They took us to this big house—'

'Where?' said Hawker.

'I'm not saying where,' said Johnny.

'And what happened?' asked Jude.

'They gave us food, and new clothes, and beds to sleep in, all right. But we couldn't get out of the house, and men in white coats watched us all the time. And they put drugs in our food.'

'How do you know that?' Hawker asked.

'I felt ill. My eyes went strange, and I couldn't see very

well. And one of the girls – she got very ill one night. She screamed and screamed, and the men in white coats came. I was in the next room and I listened through the wall. "This is very strange," one of the men said. "She

'I was in the next room and I listened through the wall.'

had 20 grams of Coplas in her dinner tonight. Was that too much, do you think?" "I don't know," said a second man. "We don't want to kill her. Let's try 20 grams again tomorrow, on this girl and on one of the boys. We can't stop this test now. We must get answers quickly." After that, they talked more quietly, and I couldn't hear. But I didn't eat any more food in that house, and the next night I got into an office downstairs and took some papers. Then I broke out of the house and ran away fast.'

'What papers?' said Hawker.

'Papers with Tyler Drug Company's name on them.'

'And where are those papers now?' asked Jude.

'That's my secret,' Johnny said. 'When the newspaper gives me the money, I'm going to tell them. But I'm not going to tell you.'

* * *

The next day Jude and Hawker flew back to Brussels and went to Arla's office. Arla listened to Johnny Cook's story, but he didn't say anything.

'So, what do we do now?' Jude said. 'Do we look for this big house and—'

Arla picked up his telephone. 'Come back in an hour,' he said. 'Get a coffee or something.'

An hour and three coffees later they went back.

'OK,' said Arla. 'You can forget all about this. Cook's story isn't true.'

Jude stared at him. 'Who told you that?' she said.

'I want to talk to Johnny Cook again,' Hawker said.

'You can't,' said Arla. 'He's dead.'

Hawker looked at Jude, and then back at Arla. 'He was alive yesterday,' said Hawker.

'Well, he isn't alive today. He came out of a club at three o'clock this morning and fell in the river Thames. When they got him out, he was dead.'

'But—' Jude began.

'Forget it, Jude. The file is closed.'

□ □ □

'And was that the end of it?' I asked, when Jude and Hawker finished telling the story.

'Yes,' said Hawker. 'Arla never spoke about it again.'

'And did you believe Johnny's story about the drug company?' I asked.

'Before a company can sell a new medicine to people,' said Hawker, 'there are years and years of tests. They do the tests on animals, of course. But they learn much more quickly from tests on people. There are lots of drug companies, and every company wants to be the first with a new medicine.'

'About five years later,' Jude said, 'the Tyler Drug

Company began to sell a new drug, called Coplastin. It was a medicine to stop some kinds of cancer, and it worked. Everybody wanted it. The company made a lot of money – and so the government got a lot of money from the company in taxes. Governments like rich companies and big, fat taxes. They're not very interested in homeless young people sleeping on the streets.'

'So Johnny Cook's story *was* true,' I said. 'And he didn't *fall* into the river – somebody pushed him.'

'Of course they pushed him,' said Jude. 'Dead men can't talk, can they?'

OMEGA FILE 451
Loch Ness, Scotland

'I want you to take the next plane to Scotland,' said Arla. 'Then get up to Loch Ness.'

'Oh, great,' said Hawker. 'Are we looking for the Loch Ness monster – old Nessie?'

Jude laughed.

'Don't laugh,' said Arla. 'You *are* looking for a monster.'

'Oh, come on, Arla,' Jude said. 'You don't mean that.'

'This photo came by email from Edinburgh,' said Arla. 'Look . . .' He turned to his computer and opened a file. 'It's a night-time photo and not very good.'

Hawker and Jude stared at the photo on the computer screen. They could see water, and something big and grey, half in and half out of the water.

'It's got arms and a head,' said Hawker. 'But what is it?'

'It kills sheep, cats, and dogs,' Arla said. 'And perhaps small children next. People in Fort Augustus are screaming at London, and London is screaming at us. Go and find it.'

'What do we do with it when we find it?' asked Jude.

'Kill it,' said Arla. 'Before it kills you.'

Hawker and Jude waited for a minute, but Arla turned away and began to read his emails.

'Are you telling us everything, Arla?' asked Hawker.

'Of course.' Arla put his hands on the table. There

'I always tell you everything,' said Arla.

were only two fingers on his left hand. 'I always tell you everything. You know that.'

'Huh!' said Jude.

* * *

They took a plane to Inverness, then drove along the side of Loch Ness to Fort Augustus. It was a grey November day – grey sky, grey water, grey hills.

Hawker looked across the loch. 'It's easy to believe in monsters here,' he said. 'Loch Ness is about 200 metres deep. The third deepest lake in Europe. Did you know that? A hundred monsters could live down there.'

'How are we going to find this thing?' asked Jude.

'Talk to people in Fort Augustus first,' Hawker said. 'Then take it from there.'

They talked to people in their hotel, and to people in the streets in Fort Augustus. Everybody had a lot to say.

'It killed Mrs Fraser's dog,' said one woman. 'She has a house down by the water. The monster came into her garden one night. Her little dog went to look, and the monster killed him – just like that.'

'Killed six of my brother's sheep,' said a man called Dugald. 'He's very angry about it.'

'Can we meet your brother?' asked Jude. 'Ask him some questions?'

Dugald's brother, Archie, lived at Invermoriston, about nine kilometres up the loch. He was a big man, with black hair and blue eyes. He was not very friendly at first.

'Who are you?' he asked. 'Are you army people?'

'No,' said Hawker. 'Why do you ask that?'

'There's an army laboratory in the hills above the loch. Lots of strange people there. And lots of boats on the loch at night. Coming and going.'

'Mmm. Interesting,' said Jude. 'But tell us about the Loch Ness monster and your dead sheep.'

'It wasn't Nessie. Nessie doesn't kill sheep,' Archie said. 'This . . . thing . . . broke their necks.'

'Did you see it?' asked Hawker.

'Well, I saw something big, but it moved very fast. It was back in the loch in seconds. And it was nearly dark.'

'Right,' said Hawker. 'Now, we'd like to look at your dead sheep, please. And then we need a boat. Where can we get a fast boat, Archie?'

'What do you want a boat for?'

'We're going to catch this thing,' said Jude, 'and stop it killing your sheep.'

For the next four days Hawker and Jude went up and down Loch Ness in Archie Campbell's boat. They talked to everybody around the loch. 'When you see this monster, please ring us. Any time. Day or night. Our mobile phones are always turned on.'

They slept a little in the day, and were out most of the

'Our mobile phones are always turned on.'

night in the boat, with their guns, cameras, mobile phones, a big flashlight, and litres of hot coffee. Once they thought they saw the monster just north of Invermoriston. Another night a call came from a little place called Foyers. They got there at six in the morning. It was dark and cold, and everything was very quiet.

They sat in the boat, looking up and down the loch.

'Look,' whispered Hawker. 'Down there, by the trees.'

Fifty metres away there were some tall trees by the side of the loch. There were some sheep under the trees – and something big and dark. Suddenly the sheep began to run.

'Start the engine,' said Hawker. 'Let's get down there.'

When they got to the trees, they found five sheep with broken necks, but no monster.

'It just kills, and goes away again,' said Jude. 'Horrible.'

The next night they were near Urquhart Castle when they saw two other boats. It was three in the morning.

'Those boats again!' said Hawker. 'We heard their engines last night. And the night before. Who are they? Let's go and see.'

Quietly, their boat moved nearer. There were four men in each boat – men in grey, young men with hard faces. They watched Hawker and Jude, and said nothing.

'Hullo,' said Jude, with a friendly smile. 'Who are you?'

A tall man in the nearest boat answered. 'Army,' he said. 'Who are you? What are you doing out here at this time of night?'

'We're visitors,' said Jude. 'Looking for Nessie, of course. What are you doing?'

'There's no monster in this loch,' said the tall man. 'Go back to your hotel and go to bed.' The two army boats moved away, down the loch.

'Nice,' said Hawker. 'Very friendly.'

Arla phoned them every morning. 'Get on with it,' he said. 'Before this thing kills someone.'

'We can't get near it,' Jude told him. 'This loch is thirty-six kilometres long and two kilometres across. There are only two of us, and we're not getting any sleep.'

'There's no monster in this loch,' said the tall man.

'You can sleep later,' said Arla. 'Just catch this thing.'

'We met some army people last night,' Jude said. 'What are they doing here? What do they do at their laboratory?'

The phone went quiet. Then, 'What laboratory?'

'The army laboratory in the hills above Loch Ness.'

The phone went dead. 'Well, well,' Jude said to Hawker. 'He doesn't know. Or he's not telling.'

The monster came out of the loch and killed sheep nearly every night. Everybody around the loch wanted to help Hawker and Jude, and their mobile phones never stopped ringing. A lot of people thought the monster was Nessie, but Archie knew it wasn't.

'Nessie never killed anything in fifteen hundred years,' he said. 'This is something different, and it's going to start killing people soon. Look, you need some sheep.'

'Sheep?' said Hawker. 'Do you mean sleep?' He was very tired after ten nights on the loch.

'Of course!' said Jude. 'Clever Archie. Can you get us some old sheep then? Or perhaps we can use Hawker. He's nearly an old sheep by now.'

'Oh, shut up,' said Hawker.

They found a good place between Invermoriston and Urquhart Castle with some trees by the water, and took their six old sheep there. For three nights they watched, but no monster came. The men in grey were out every

They found a good place with some trees by the water,
and took their six old sheep there.

night too. They were never far away from Hawker and
Jude, but never came to speak to them.

On the fourth night Hawker and Jude arrived at their
sheep place later than usual. It was a warm, rainy night –
soft Scottish rain that never stops.

When they turned the engine off, everything was quiet
– just the rain whispering on the loch. Hawker got out of
the boat and stood with the flashlight, watching and
listening. Jude sat in the boat, with her gun in her hand.

21

'Where are the men in grey?' whispered Hawker.

'Don't know,' Jude whispered back. 'Behind us, I think.'

Then everything happened at once. There was a sudden noise of boats' engines behind them, and at the same time something moved in the water in front of them. A head and two long arms came out of the water.

'Light!' shouted Jude. 'Quick!'

Hawker turned on the flashlight, and at once the monster stood up and ran at Hawker through the water, its long arms going for Hawker's head.

'Get down, Hawker!' screamed Jude. In a second Hawker was under the water, and then came the sound of Jude's gun – once, twice, and then a third time.

When the monster stopped moving, Hawker and Jude went to look at it. It was a greeny-black colour, bigger than a man, and with very long arms and legs. It had a small head on a long neck. It was a strange, horrible thing.

A minute later, the men in grey arrived in their two boats. They got out and came to look at the dead monster.

'Oh dear,' the tall man said. 'Poor old Nessie.'

'That', said Hawker, 'is *not* Nessie. So what is it?'

'Visitors, aren't you?' said the tall man. 'Where from?'

Hawker and Jude stared at him and said nothing. Then

'*Get down, Hawker!*' *screamed Jude.*

Jude took something out of her pocket and held it up, in front of the tall man's eyes.

He looked at it. 'Oh,' he said. 'I see. EDI. Don't see many of those. OK, what do you want to know?'

'What – is – that – *thing*?' said Jude.

The tall man looked unhappy. 'It is, or it was, one of

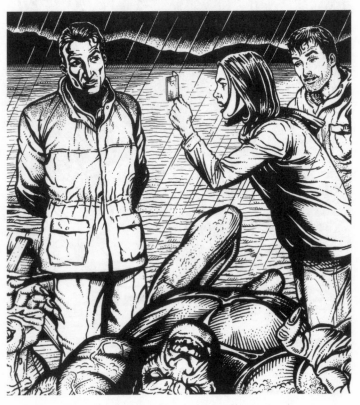

Jude held it up, in front of the tall man's eyes.

24

the army's new fighters. It got away from our laboratory, and we just couldn't catch it.'

'But it was alive . . . a – a living thing,' said Hawker.

'You can make a lot of living things in a laboratory these days,' said the tall man. 'Genetic engineering is getting very clever. This fighter can run all night, live under water, see in the dark. But it's new. We haven't got it right yet.'

'And it's programmed to kill anything, is it?' said Jude.

'No, no,' the tall man said quickly. 'Not this one. This one just kills small animals with four legs – sheep, dogs, cats, things like that.'

'Well,' said Jude, 'that *is* nice to know.'

'And where are the other monsters?' asked Hawker. 'For killing men, women, and children – things like that.'

The tall man smiled. 'Can't answer that, I'm afraid. Talk to your people in Brussels. Well, we must get back. Lots to do, you know. Thanks for your help. Bye.'

The men in grey put their dead monster in one of the boats and went away up the loch into the dark and the rain.

□ □ □

'And what did Arla say about it all?' I asked.

'He was so angry!' Hawker said. 'He went crazy! He

didn't know about the monsters, you see. Or the laboratory. The army didn't tell anyone in Brussels.'

'And Arla liked to know everyone's secrets,' said Jude.

'Did the army make any more monsters?' I asked.

'Not in Scotland,' said Hawker. 'The British army closed their laboratory after that. The Americans and the French made some monsters years later. They were smaller, like big cats, but with eight legs.'

'Where are they now?' I said. 'You don't hear anything about them.'

'Of course not,' said Jude. 'People don't want to hear about monsters.'

'They're in Antarctica. Or in a place deep under the ground,' said Hawker. 'Nice and secret. Just waiting for the next war.'

'And so there isn't a Loch Ness monster, and never was one,' I said.

'Nessie?' said Jude. She looked me in the eyes and did not smile. 'Of course there's a Loch Ness monster. She's a blue-grey colour, has a small head, a very long neck, and is about fifteen metres long . . . Go and look at all the photos of her on the Internet.'

OMEGA FILE 522
Galápagos, Ecuador

'Got your sun hats?' said Arla.

'Why?' asked Jude. 'Where are we going now?'

'South America,' Arla said.

'Big place,' said Jude. 'How about Chile? I like Chile.'

'No, it's Ecuador. You're going to the Galápagos Islands, a thousand kilometres out in the Pacific Ocean.'

'Oh, right,' Hawker said. 'Are you going to tell us why?'

Arla looked unhappy. 'There's something strange going on. EDI is getting emails every day from the Galápagos. They're all about Isabela Island and they all say things like this.' He gave Hawker and Jude a piece of paper.

> ***IMPORTANT NEWS***IMPORTANT NEWS***
> A new time is coming for our planet.
> The first visitors are now on Isabela Island, Galápagos.
> Don't fight them.   Don't be afraid of them.   Be friendly.
> Tell your government now.

Hawker and Jude looked at Arla, and then laughed. 'There are a lot of crazy people out there on the Internet,' said Jude. 'You don't believe this one – do you?'

'Perhaps it's crazy, and perhaps it's not,' said Arla. 'But when we email back with questions, they don't answer. The Americans are watching the island by satellite, but they don't want to tell us why. There are two Australian ships going there. The Mexicans are getting very excited, and the Ecuadorians are saying nothing . . . *Something* is happening on Isabela. What is it? We want to know.'

* * *

From Brussels to the Galápagos is a long way. Hawker and Jude took a plane to Cuba, a second plane to Ecuador, then a third plane out to Baltra Island, in the Galápagos. When they got out of the plane, a wall of hot air hit them.

'Whew,' said Hawker. He put on his sun hat quickly.

They went across to Santa Cruz Island and down to Puerto Ayora. There they found a boat, the *Sea-Lion*, to take them to Isabela, about 90 kilometres away. At first, the boatman, Gonzalo, did not want to take them.

'My boat can take ten people,' he said. 'It's a very good boat, but very expensive for only two people.'

Jude smiled at him. 'Not for two rich people.'

'Rich?' said Hawker. 'It's not our money – ouch!'

Jude hit him hard on the arm. 'We're on holiday,' she told Gonzalo. 'We want to see the giant tortoises on Isabela.' She looked at Hawker. 'Don't we?'

'Er, yes. That's right,' said Hawker quickly. 'We're very interested in the giant tortoises.'

On the way to Isabela Island Jude read a book about the Galápagos, and Hawker watched the sea. 'Isabela is a very young island,' Jude told him. 'And it has – listen to this! – *six* volcanoes. One erupted only two years ago.'

'Oh, that's great!' said Hawker. 'Crazy emails, strange visitors in the middle of the Pacific, and now erupting volcanoes! Thank you, Arla!'

Not many people lived on Isabela, and Puerto Villamil was usually a sleepy place. But when the *Sea-Lion* arrived, there were about fifty people down by the sea. There were two small boats, and on them Hawker and

'Isabela has six *volcanoes,' said Jude.*

Jude could see chairs and tables, beds, boxes and bags, and a bicycle.

Gonzalo called out in Spanish to the people on the boats, then turned to Hawker and Jude. 'Lots of people are leaving Isabela,' he said. 'They are afraid.'

'Afraid of what?' asked Jude. 'Go and talk to them, Hawker. Your Spanish is better than mine.'

Hawker came back half an hour later. 'You're not going to believe this,' he told Jude. 'The people here say

'Lots of people are leaving Isabela. They are afraid.'

30

there's a spaceship on Isabela. It came down ten days ago, right down inside Volcano Alcedo. And it's still there.'

'How do they know that?' said Jude.

'There's an Australian, Dr Jim Miller, up on Alcedo. He works here, studying giant tortoises. He saw the spaceship, and now he's waiting for the visitors to come out.'

'So the "visitors" in those emails are extraterrestrials. ETs. Little green men from another planet. Oh dear,' said Jude. 'Can we go home now, Hawker?'

Hawker laughed. 'No, we can't. We climb Volcano Alcedo,' he said. 'Talk to Dr Miller. Say hello to the ETs.'

'Oh dear,' Jude said again. 'I was afraid of that.'

Gonzalo took them in the *Sea-Lion* up to Shipton Cove. There, very early the next morning, Hawker and Jude began their climb up the volcano.

'There is a path,' Gonzalo told them, 'but it is five hours to the top and hard climbing. And very, very hot. You must carry water – two litres for one person for one day. You must sleep at the top and come down tomorrow – but not when the sun is high in the sky. And be careful, please!'

'Careful of the spaceship visitors, you mean?' said Jude.

31

'I don't know about spaceships,' smiled Gonzalo, 'but Volcano Alcedo is always a little excited – she is always doing something new.'

It was a very hard climb. After two hours, they stopped under some trees. They drank some water and looked out over the blue sea. The black volcanic rocks under their feet were hot from the sun.

'It's so beautiful here,' said Jude.

'Mmm. Yes and no,' said Hawker. Then, 'Hey, Jude! Look! That animal, over there by that rock. What – is – it?'

'Oh, wow!' whispered Jude. 'It's an iguana – a Galápagos iguana. Isn't he wonderful?'

The iguana stared at them with its hot orange eyes, and did not move. Its body was about a metre long, and an orange-yellowy colour.

'It looks about a thousand years old,' said Hawker. 'A very strange animal.'

'Everything about this island is strange,' said Jude.

They climbed and climbed, and the sun got hotter and hotter. After three more hours they came to the top, and looked down into the great crater of Alcedo, two hundred metres deep and seven kilometres across. To the north and the south they could see more volcanoes, and across the sea to the west the island of Fernandina – but they could not see Dr Miller or his camp.

'We need to go round the crater to the south,' said

Hawker. 'It's another two hours' walk, the villagers said.'

It was hard walking over the black lava rock, and once Hawker nearly fell. Jude caught his arm.

'Don't break a leg here,' she said. 'I don't want to carry you back down to the boat.'

'Why not?' said Hawker. 'I carried you home once.'

'We weren't on top of a volcano then,' said Jude.

At last they saw Dr Miller's camp, and ten minutes

The iguana stared at them with its hot orange eyes.

later they arrived. Dr Miller was short, very brown, and angry.

'Go away!' he shouted. 'You're Americans, aren't you?'

'No, we aren't,' said Hawker. 'We're European. How do you do, Dr Miller?'

'What are you doing here?' he said angrily.

'We'd like to talk to you,' said Jude quietly. 'About the spaceship down in the crater. Why are you so angry?'

'Because nobody listens to me!' said Dr Miller. 'Nobody believes me! The Americans say, "Oh, crazy man!". The Australian government says, "Get some sleep!" What can I do? Something very important is happening on this planet, and nobody is listening!'

'Well, we're here now, and we're listening,' Jude said.

Dr Miller looked at them. 'Who do you work for?'

'Europe,' said Hawker. 'Europe is very interested in this spaceship. Please tell us about it.'

'Ah, the emails did get through, then,' said Dr Miller.

'Who did the emails come from?' asked Hawker.

'Ecuadorian friends,' said Dr Miller. 'Over on Santa Cruz. Look, I've got some beer here. You want one?'

They sat on the black lava rocks under the hot sun, and drank hot beer. Below them clouds of smoke and steam moved this way and that way across the crater. And was there, under those clouds, a spaceship from another planet?

They sat on the black lava rocks, and drank hot beer.

'Sometimes I think I can see it down there,' said Jim Miller, 'but mostly I can't. It's a great white thing, and long legs came out of it when it came down.'

'But why here, Jim?' said Jude. 'Why into a volcano?'

'Who knows?' said Jim. 'Perhaps they like hot places. Perhaps they need something from the hot lava.'

'And why are you angry with the Americans, Jim?' Hawker asked. 'I know their beer's no good, but . . .'

'They watched this spaceship on their satellite. I know
they did. They *know* it's here, but they don't want the
world to know. They don't want people like you and me
to meet any extraterrestrial visitors. Oh no! They want it
all to be a big secret. Then they can be top dog.'

Just then there was a sudden noise, a BOOM deep below
the ground. 'What . . . what was that, Jim?' asked Jude.

'Oh, Alcedo does that all the time,' said Jim. 'Then hot
water comes up, and steam, dust − sometimes a little
lava, but not much. That's why there are always clouds
in the crater. You can never see anything down there.'

'Can we climb down into the crater?' asked Hawker.

'Are you crazy? It's dangerous down there!' Jim said.

All evening Hawker and Jude stared down into the
crater, but they could see nothing through the clouds of
steam and dust. Just before the sun went down, Hawker
saw something near the top of the crater and shouted to
Jude, but it was only two of the giant tortoises. They
came slowly past the camp and went away down the
other side of the volcano. Later, four more came past,
going the same way, moving slowly and quietly over the
black rocks.

'They're very strange animals!' said Jude.

Hawker and Jude did not sleep much. The rocks were
hard, and below them they heard again and again the
deep BOOM of the volcano. Late in the night they turned

their radio on. It was very noisy, but through the noise they could hear a voice from Santa Cruz. Hawker listened hard.

'They're talking about Volcano Alcedo!' he said. 'They think it's going to erupt in the next twenty-four hours!'

Jude sat up. 'Oh no! We're seven hours away from the boat. Let's get moving! Go and call Jim.'

But Jim Miller did not believe Santa Cruz radio. 'It's the Americans again,' he said. 'They want us all to go away.'

The giant tortoises came slowly past the camp.

'Please come with us, Jim,' said Jude. 'Please. You can come back in a day or two.'

'You two go,' said Jim, 'but I'm staying right here, and watching that spaceship.'

It was a hard climb down. When they got to the sea, they saw Gonzalo with the little boat. 'Hurry!' he shouted. 'Did you hear on the radio? Alcedo's going to erupt!'

Quickly, they went out to the *Sea-Lion* and climbed up onto the boat. 'Go! Go! Go!' Gonzalo shouted to his men, and before long the *Sea-Lion* was a kilometre out at sea.

Two hours later Volcano Alcedo erupted. There was a sudden great BANG! – and then clouds of dust flew up into the sky. Red-hot lava came out of the volcano's sides and ran down to the sea. The noise did not stop, and with every bang, rocks flew hundreds of metres up into the sky, then fell slowly back down to the ground. For hours the night sky was filled with great flowers of red and orange light.

It was a beautiful, and a terrifying thing to watch.

□ □ □

'What happened to Dr Miller?' I asked.

'Poor Jim went to the great spaceship in the sky,'

Two hours later Volcano Alcedo erupted.

Jude said. 'Five hundred metres of red-hot lava fell on top of him.'

'And was there a spaceship in the volcano?'

'No,' said Jude.

'Yes,' said Hawker.

He looked at Jude, and they laughed. Then Jude looked at me. 'What do you want to believe?' she asked. 'They weren't very clever extraterrestrials, were they? – sitting there in their spaceship in an erupting volcano!'

Hawker smiled. 'Ah, but perhaps the spaceship left just before the volcano erupted. Gonzalo and I saw something in the clouds of dust – a white light, moving very fast, faster than the dust. It went up very high.'

'Well, I didn't see anything,' said Jude. 'And that's because there wasn't anything in that volcano!'

Hawker looked up into the blue Greek sky. 'How do we know?' he said slowly. 'One day someone, or something, is going to visit us from out there. Perhaps that was the first visit, all those years ago in the Galápagos. Who knows?'

GLOSSARY

army   all the soldiers of a country
believe   to think that something is true or real
camp   a place where people live in tents for a short time
cancer   a dangerous illness
catch (past tense **caught**)   to find and hold someone or something
clever   quick to learn, understand or do something
cloud   a white or grey thing in the sky (rain comes from clouds)
club / go clubbing   to go dancing in a dance club at night
crater   a very large hole in the top of a volcano
crazy   mad (ill in the head) or very stupid
dance *(v)*   to move the body to music
dangerous   something that is dangerous can hurt or kill you
drug company   a company that makes medicines
dust *(n)*   dry dirt that is like powder
earring   something that you wear on your ear
email   a way of sending a 'letter' or message by computer
engine   a machine that makes things move (e.g. a car engine)
erupt   when a volcano erupts, very hot liquid rock comes out
Euro   money used in some European countries
extraterrestrial (**ET**)   a 'person' from another planet
fall (past tense **fell**)   to go down quickly; to drop
fight *(v)*   to try to hurt or kill someone
file   a place to keep information (on paper, on a computer, etc.)
flashlight   a light that you can carry in the hand
genetic engineering   changing the information in genes to make
     plants, animals, etc. change or grow differently
government   a group of people who control a country
homeless   without a home

horrible   very bad; making you feel afraid
intelligence (**department of**)   the part of a government that
    collects secret information
laboratory   a room or building where scientists work
lava   very hot liquid rock that comes out of a volcano
loch   a Scottish word for a lake
medicine   something that helps you get better when you are ill
mobile phone   a telephone that works by radio; you can carry it
    with you and use it anywhere
monster   a very big, strange, frightening animal
path   a little 'road' where people can walk
planet   a large round thing in space that moves around a star
programmed   told by a computer program to do something
rock *(n)*   the hard part of the ground
satellite   a thing (made by people) in space; it moves around the
    Earth and sends back radio messages or television pictures
scream *(v)*   to make a loud high cry when you are afraid or hurt
secret   something that other people must not know
shout *(v)*   to speak or call out in a very loud voice
spaceship   a special kind of 'aeroplane' that can travel in space
stare *(v)*   to look at something for a long time
steam *(n)*   when water gets very hot, it changes into steam
strange   very unusual or surprising
tax   money that you must pay to the government
terrifying   very, very frightening
test *(n)*   using or looking at something (e. g. a new medicine)
    very carefully, to learn about it
tortoise / giant tortoise   an animal with a hard shell on its back,
    that moves very slowly ('giant' is very, very big)
volcano (*adj* **volcanic**)   a mountain with a hole in the top
whisper *(v)*   to speak very, very quietly

The Omega Files

SHORT STORIES

ACTIVITIES

Before Reading

1 **Read the back cover of the book, and the introduction on the first page. What do you know now about these stories? Tick one box for each sentence.**

	YES	NO
1 Hawker and Jude travel all over the world.	☐	☐
2 They work for the American Department of Intelligence.	☐	☐
3 The Omega Files are in all the newspapers.	☐	☐
4 There are some surprising stories in the files.	☐	☐
5 Hawker and Jude write for a newspaper.	☐	☐
6 Hawker and Jude always find the answers.	☐	☐

2 **What is going to happen in these stories? Can you guess? Use this table to make some sentences.**

Hawker and Jude . . .

find	a monster	
climb	little green men	
talk to	a high mountain	in London
kill	a young man	on a Pacific island
go dancing with	a dangerous drug	in a spaceship
go swimming with	a crazy Australian	in Scotland
travel with	a volcano	

While Reading

Read about *EDI* and then read *Omega File 349*. Are these sentences true (T) or false (F)? Rewrite the false ones with the correct information.

1 Johnny Cook went swimming nearly every day.
2 When they left the last club, Hawker and Jude took Johnny Cook to their house for dinner.
3 Johnny Cook wanted to sell a story about a drug company to a newspaper.
4 The company used homeless people for language tests.
5 Johnny Cook knew about this because he listened through the wall.
6 Hawker wanted to talk to Johnny Cook again.
7 Hawker and Jude couldn't talk to Johnny Cook again because he was in New York.

At the end of the story, Arla says 'Forget it,' so Hawker and Jude can't ask questions. What questions would you like them to ask Arla? Use these words to make some questions.

- Who . . . (be / with Johnny Cook / when / fall / river)?
- Who . . . (find / Johnny Cook's body / river)?
- Who . . . (you / telephone / when / we / go / coffee)?
- Who . . . (say / Johnny Cook's story / not / true)?

Read *Omega File 451: Loch Ness, Scotland* down to the bottom of page 21. Choose the best question-word for these questions, and then answer them.

How / What

1 . . . did people around the loch help Hawker and Jude?
2 . . . did Hawker and Jude do every night?
3 . . . did the men in grey want Hawker and Jude to do?
4 . . . did the monster do nearly every night?
5 . . . did Archie Campbell help Hawker and Jude?

Before you finish reading *Omega File 451*, can you guess how the story ends? Which of these endings do you like best? Tick all the ones you like.

1 The men in grey catch the monster and take it away before Hawker and Jude can see it.
2 Hawker and Jude catch the monster and take it to Arla.
3 The monster kills one of the men in grey.
4 Jude shoots the monster and kills it.
5 Hawker and Jude go to the army laboratory and find a lot more monsters there.
6 Arla phones and says, 'Come back to Brussels and forget the monster.' Hawker and Jude don't know why.
7 The monster is something made by the army.
8 The monster is something from another planet.
9 The monster really *is* Nessie, the Loch Ness monster.

ACTIVITIES: *While Reading*

Read *Omega File 522: Galápagos, Ecuador* down to the bottom of page 37. Then match these halves of sentences to make five sentences.

1 Arla wanted Hawker and Jude to go to Isabela Island . . .
2 Dr Miller was very angry with everybody . . .
3 Hawker and Jude stared down into the crater . . .
4 In the night they listened to the radio . . .
5 They wanted Dr Miller to go with them to the boat, . . .

6 and heard the news about Volcano Alcedo erupting.
7 because he had strange emails about visitors there.
8 but Dr Miller did not believe the news on the radio.
9 but they could not see anything through the clouds of steam and dust down there.
10 because nobody believed his stories about the spaceship.

Before you finish reading *Omega File 522*, can you guess the answers to these questions?

1 Does Jim Miller go to the boat with Hawker and Jude?
2 Does the volcano erupt?
3 Do Hawker and Jude get to the boat before the volcano erupts?
4 Does anybody get killed?
5 Does Jim Miller leave the island in the spaceship?
6 Do Hawker and Jude both see the spaceship?
7 Is it possible that there really *is* a spaceship?

After Reading

1 **What did Jude say to Arla after the visit to Scotland? Put their conversation in the right order and write in the speakers' names. Arla speaks first (number 3).**

1 _____ 'And the army is even more dangerous! I'm going to close their laboratory.'

2 _____ 'It can run all night, live under water, see in the dark, and it kills small animals with four legs.'

3 _____ 'OK, Jude. Tell me about it. What was it?'

4 _____ 'No, of course he hasn't. This monster isn't very clever, Arla, but it's horrible – and dangerous.'

5 _____ 'Mm. Genetic engineering. And what can it do?'

6 _____ 'Good. Please do it soon, Arla!'

7 _____ 'It was one of the army's new fighters. It was a living thing – half animal, half person.'

8 _____ 'But why did it try to kill Hawker then? Hawker hasn't got four legs.'

2 **Circle the best words to complete Hawker's email to Arla.**

Before / *When* the volcano erupted, I saw a *light* / *rock* in the sky, moving *down* / *up* very fast. Jude says it *was not* / *was* a spaceship, but it moved *more slowly* / *faster* than the clouds of *lava* / *dust*. So what was it?

48

3 Use the clues below to complete this crossword with words from the story. Then find the hidden ten-letter word in the crossword. Is this word a place, a person, or an animal?

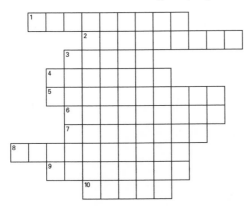

1 You can read the news in a _____ every day.

2 It is _____ to climb down into a volcano.

3 A company must do many _____ before they can sell a new medicine.

4 When a _____ erupts, lava and red-hot rock come out.

5 A special room for scientists to work in.

6 You can travel to planets and stars in a _____.

7 This animal moves very, very slowly.

8 When you look for something in the dark, you need a _____.

9 When you are ill, you take _____ to make you better.

10 A letter sent by computer.

The hidden word is _____, and it is _____.

4 Here is a new illustration for one of the stories. Find the best place for it, and answer these questions.

The picture goes on page _____, in the story _____.

1 Where are Hawker and Jude?
2 What is the voice on the radio saying?
3 What do Hawker and Jude do next?

Now write a caption for the illustration.

Caption: _____

5 Here are some new titles for the three stories. Which titles go with which stories? Some titles are good (G); some titles are not good (NG). Can you explain why?

Crazy Dr Miller   Hullo, Planet Earth!

Danger on the Streets   The Men in Grey

An Army for the Future   Drugs for the Homeless

A Nice Friendly Monster   Listening Through the Wall

Danger from the Sky   The Volcano Spaceship

Johnny   Danger in the Water

6 Are the things in these stories possible? Perhaps not today, but perhaps in the future? What do you think? Tick some boxes in this table.

POSSIBLE . . .	TODAY?	IN 10 YEARS?	IN 100 YEARS?	NEVER!
Using homeless people for drugs tests				
Making monsters to fight in armies				
Spaceships visiting from other planets				

7 What did you think about these stories? Complete these sentences with your ideas.

1 I felt sorry for _____ when _____.

2 I didn't like it when _____.

3 I liked *Omega File* _____ best because _____.

51

ABOUT THE AUTHOR

Jennifer Bassett has worked in English Language Teaching since 1972. She has been a teacher, teacher trainer, editor, and materials writer, and has taught in England, Greece, Spain, and Portugal. She is the current Series Editor of the Oxford Bookworms Library, and has written several other stories for the series, including *One-Way Ticket* and *The President's Murderer* (both at Stage 1). She lives and works in Devonshire, in the south-west of England.

She has been to Loch Ness in Scotland and heard stories about the Loch Ness monster, but she has not seen Nessie herself. And when she went to Isabela Island in the Galápagos, she did not see a spaceship in the crater of a volcano. But there were a lot of clouds that day . . .

OXFORD BOOKWORMS LIBRARY

Classics • Crime & Mystery • Factfiles • Fantasy & Horror
Human Interest • Playscripts • Thriller & Adventure
True Stories • World Stories

The OXFORD BOOKWORMS LIBRARY provides enjoyable reading in English, with a wide range of classic and modern fiction, non-fiction, and plays. It includes original and adapted texts in seven carefully graded language stages, which take learners from beginner to advanced level. An overview is given on the next pages.

All Stage 1 titles are available as audio recordings, as well as over eighty other titles from Starter to Stage 6. All Starters and many titles at Stages 1 to 4 are specially recommended for younger learners. Every Bookworm is illustrated, and Starters and Factfiles have full-colour illustrations.

The OXFORD BOOKWORMS LIBRARY also offers extensive support. Each book contains an introduction to the story, notes about the author, a glossary, and activities. Additional resources include tests and worksheets, and answers for these and for the activities in the books. There is advice on running a class library, using audio recordings, and the many ways of using Oxford Bookworms in reading programmes. Resource materials are available on the website <www.oup.com/bookworms>.

The *Oxford Bookworms Collection* is a series for advanced learners. It consists of volumes of short stories by well-known authors, both classic and modern. Texts are not abridged or adapted in any way, but carefully selected to be accessible to the advanced student.

You can find details and a full list of titles in the *Oxford Bookworms Library Catalogue* and *Oxford English Language Teaching Catalogues*, and on the website <www.oup.com/bookworms>.

THE OXFORD BOOKWORMS LIBRARY
GRADING AND SAMPLE EXTRACTS

STARTER • 250 HEADWORDS

present simple – present continuous – imperative –
can/cannot, must – *going to* (future) – simple gerunds ...

Her phone is ringing – but where is it?

Sally gets out of bed and looks in her bag. No phone. She looks under the bed. No phone. Then she looks behind the door. There is her phone. Sally picks up her phone and answers it. *Sally's Phone*

STAGE 1 • 400 HEADWORDS

... past simple – coordination with *and*, *but*, *or* –
subordination with *before*, *after*, *when*, *because*, *so* ...

I knew him in Persia. He was a famous builder and I worked with him there. For a time I was his friend, but not for long. When he came to Paris, I came after him – I wanted to watch him. He was a very clever, very dangerous man. *The Phantom of the Opera*

STAGE 2 • 700 HEADWORDS

... present perfect – *will* (future) – *(don't) have to, must not, could* –
comparison of adjectives – simple *if* clauses – past continuous –
tag questions – *ask/tell* + infinitive ...

While I was writing these words in my diary, I decided what to do. I must try to escape. I shall try to get down the wall outside. The window is high above the ground, but I have to try. I shall take some of the gold with me – if I escape, perhaps it will be helpful later. *Dracula*

... should, may – present perfect continuous – *used to* – past perfect –
causative – relative clauses – indirect statements ...

Of course, it was most important that no one should see
Colin, Mary, or Dickon entering the secret garden. So Colin
gave orders to the gardeners that they must all keep away
from that part of the garden in future. ***The Secret Garden***

STAGE 4 • 1400 HEADWORDS

... past perfect continuous – passive (simple forms) –
would conditional clauses – indirect questions –
relatives with *where/when* – gerunds after prepositions/phrases ...

I was glad. Now Hyde could not show his face to the world
again. If he did, every honest man in London would be proud
to report him to the police. ***Dr Jekyll and Mr Hyde***

STAGE 5 • 1800 HEADWORDS

... future continuous – future perfect –
passive (modals, continuous forms) –
would have conditional clauses – modals + perfect infinitive ...

If he had spoken Estella's name, I would have hit him. I was so
angry with him, and so depressed about my future, that I could
not eat the breakfast. Instead I went straight to the old house.
Great Expectations

STAGE 6 • 2500 HEADWORDS

... passive (infinitives, gerunds) – advanced modal meanings –
clauses of concession, condition

When I stepped up to the piano, I was confident. It was as if I
knew that the prodigy side of me really did exist. And when I
started to play, I was so caught up in how lovely I looked that
I didn't worry how I would sound. ***The Joy Luck Club***

The Monkey's Paw

W. W. JACOBS

Retold by Diane Mowat

Outside, the night is cold and wet. Inside, the White family sits and waits. Where is their visitor?

There is a knock at the door. A man is standing outside in the dark. Their visitor has arrived.

The visitor waits. He has been in India for many years. What has he got? He has brought the hand of a small, dead animal – a monkey's paw.

Outside, in the dark, the visitor smiles and waits for the door to open.

Ned Kelly: A True Story

CHRISTINE LINDOP

When he was a boy, he was poor and hungry. When he was a young man, he was still poor and still hungry. He learnt how to steal horses, he learnt how to fight, he learnt how to live – outside the law. Australia in the 1870s was a hard, wild place. Rich people had land, poor people didn't. So the rich got richer, and the poor stayed poor.

Some say Ned Kelly was a bad man. Some say he was a good man but the law was bad. This is the true story of Australia's most famous outlaw.